charlie parker

Arranged by Brent Edstrom

contents

Cover photo: William P. Gottlieb Collection/Library of Congress

ISBN 978-1-4950-3082-6

HAL•LEONARD®
CORPORATION

7777 W. BLUEMOUND RD. P.O. BOX 13819 MILWAUKEE, WI 53213

For all works contained herein:
Unauthorized copying, arranging, adapting, recording, Internet posting, public performance,
or other distribution of the printed music in this publication is an infringement of copyright.
Infringers are liable under the law.

Visit Hal Leonard Online at
www.halleonard.com

APRIL IN PARIS

Words by E.Y. "YIP" HARBURG
Music by VERNON DUKE

Arrangement based on a performance by Charlie Parker

Copyright © 1932 by Kay Duke Music and Glocca Morra Music LLC
Copyright Renewed
This arrangement Copyright © 2016 by Kay Duke Music and Glocca Morra Music LLC
All Rights for Kay Duke Music Administered by Universal Music Corp.
All Rights for Glocca Morra Music LLC Administered by Shapiro, Bernstein & Co., Inc.
International Copyright Secured   All Rights Reserved

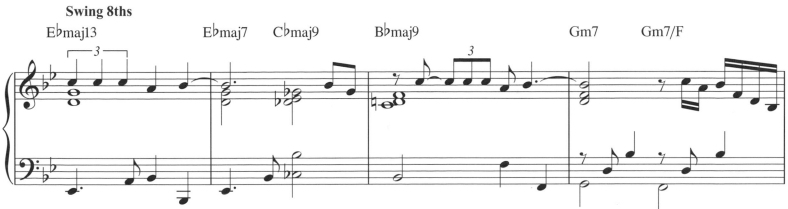

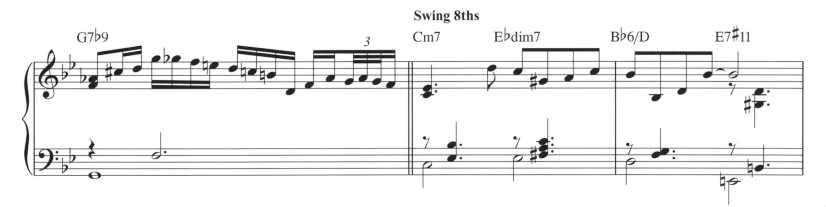

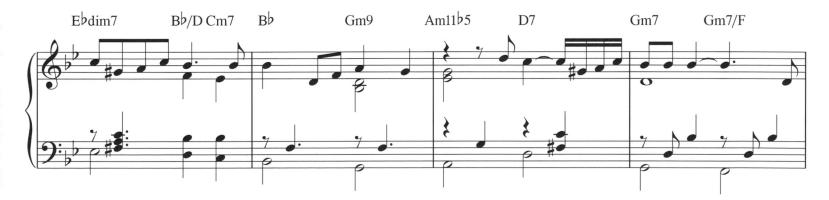

4

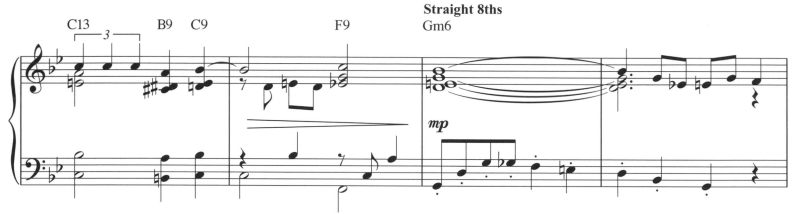

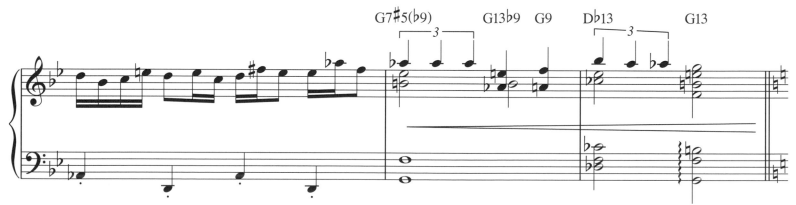

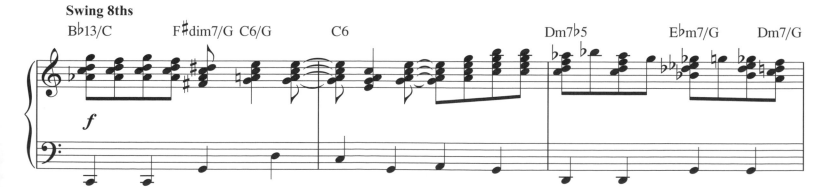

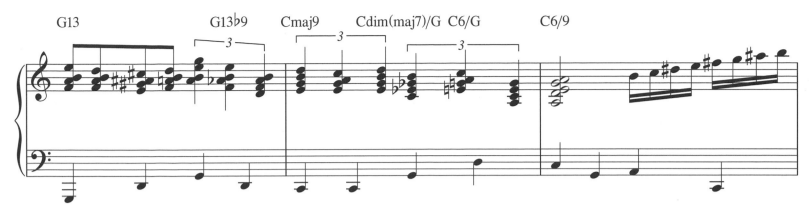

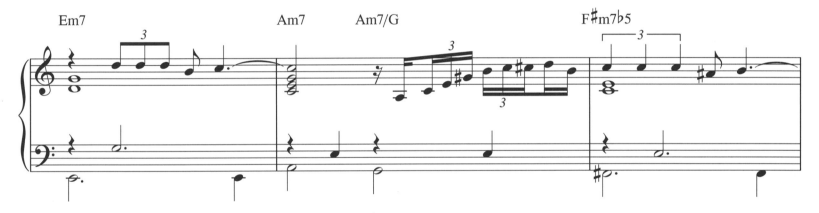

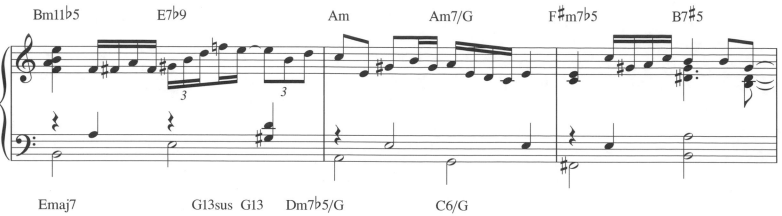

Straight 8ths

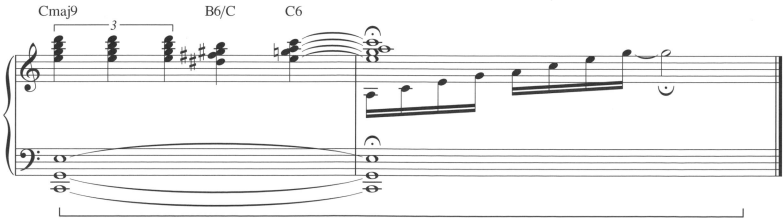

AU PRIVAVE

By CHARLIE PARKER

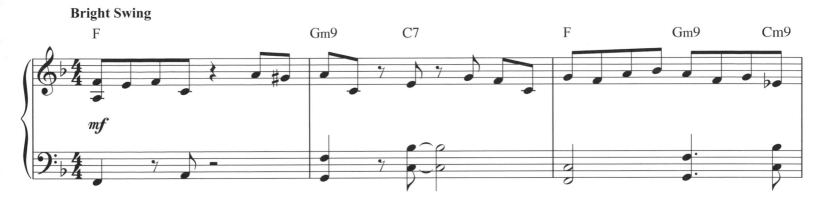

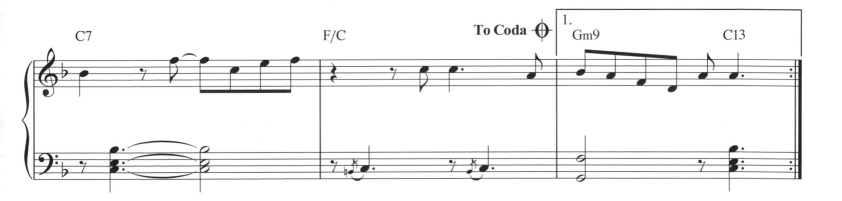

Copyright © 1956 (Renewed 1984) Atlantic Music Corp.
This arrangement Copyright © 2016 Atlantic Music Corp.
International Copyright Secured   All Rights Reserved

Solo based on ones by Charlie Parker and Dizzy Gillespie

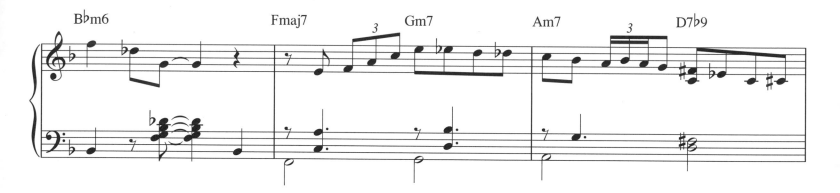

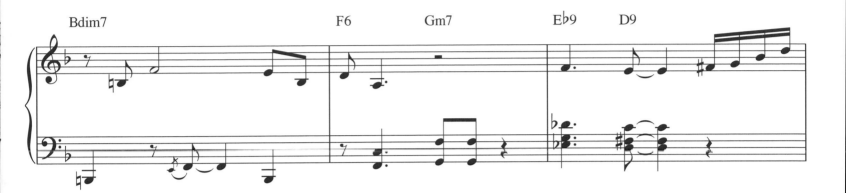

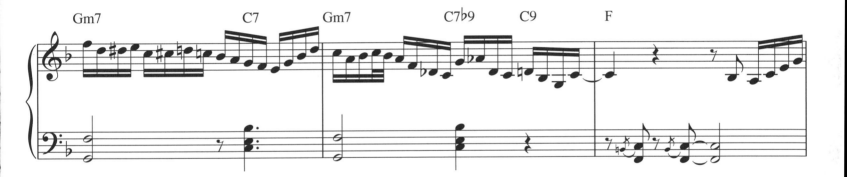

Gm7   C7   F   B♭   Bdim

F   Cm7   F7   B♭7

Fmaj7   Gm7   Am7   A♭m7   Gm7

D.C. al Coda

C7   F7♯11   Gm7   C9

CODA

Gm9   Fmaj7

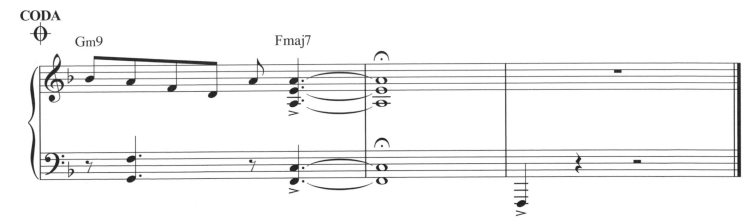

BILLIE'S BOUNCE
(Bill's Bounce)

Moderate Swing

By CHARLIE PARKER

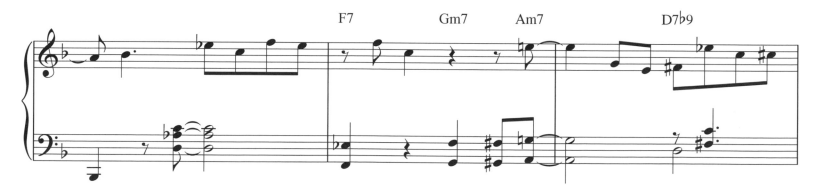

Copyright © 1945 (Renewed 1973) Atlantic Music Corp.
This arrangement Copyright © 2016 Atlantic Music Corp.
All Rights for the World excluding the U.S. Controlled and Administered by Screen Gems-EMI Music Inc.
International Copyright Secured   All Rights Reserved

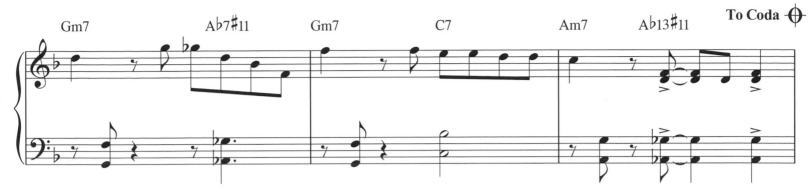

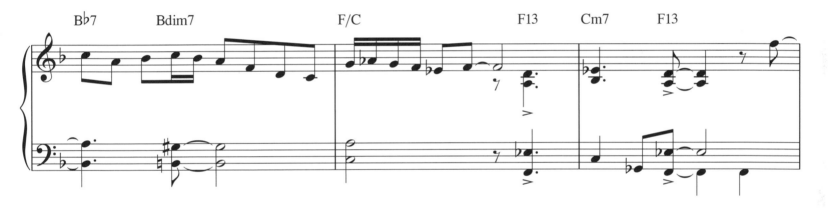

Solo based on one by Charlie Parker

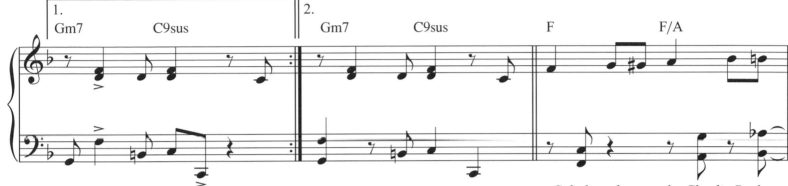

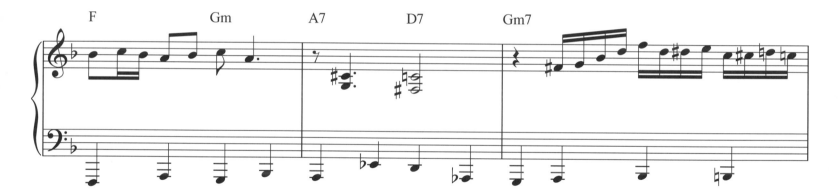

D.S. al Coda

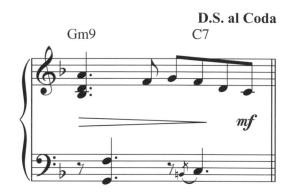

CODA

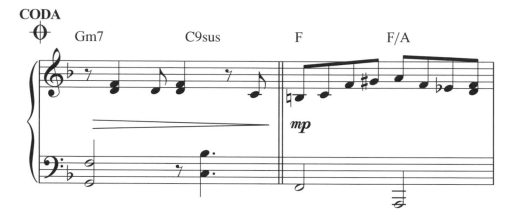

CONFIRMATION

By CHARLIE PARKER

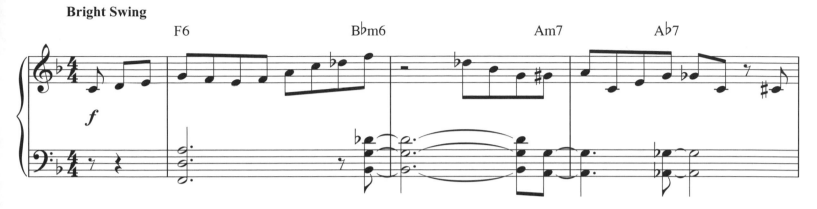

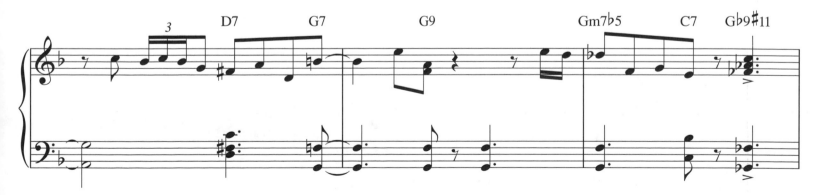

Copyright © 1946 (Renewed 1974) Atlantic Music Corp.
This arrangement Copyright © 2016 Atlantic Music Corp.
International Copyright Secured   All Rights Reserved

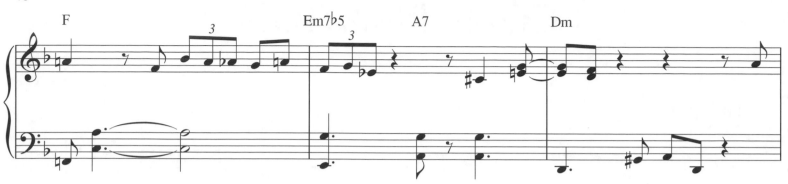

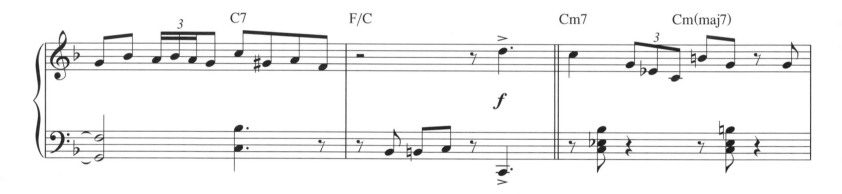

Solo based on one by Charlie Parker

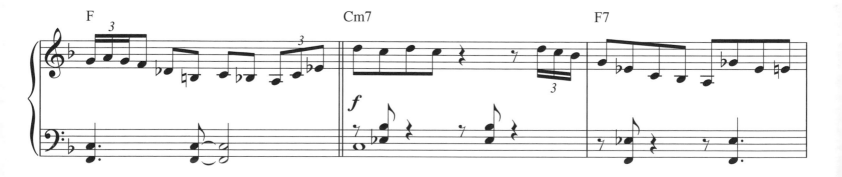

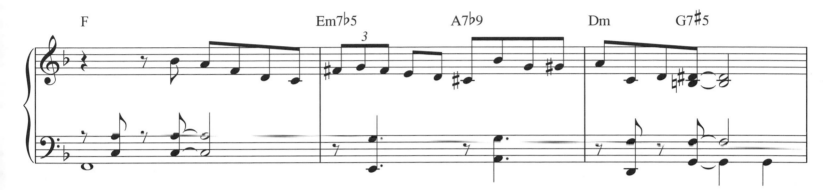

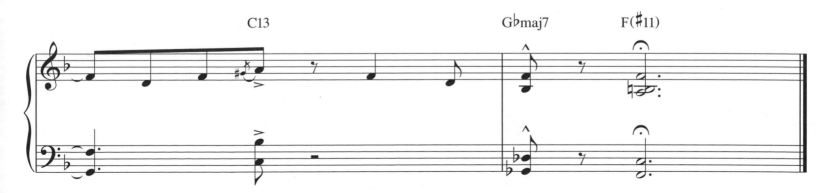

BLOOMDIDO

By CHARLIE PARKER

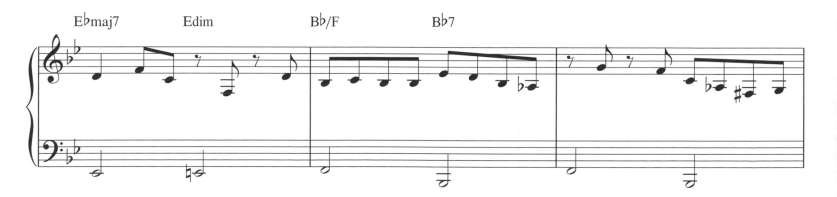

Copyright © 1953 (Renewed 1981) Atlantic Music Corp.
This arrangement Copyright © 2016 Atlantic Music Corp.
International Copyright Secured   All Rights Reserved

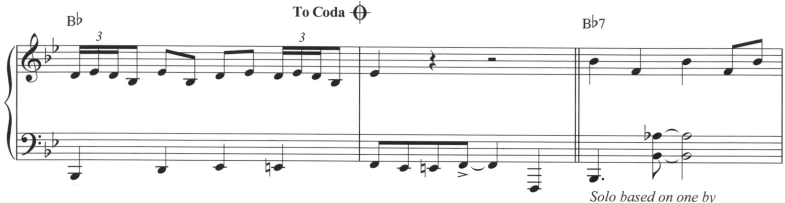

To Coda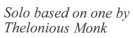

Solo based on one by Thelonious Monk

DEWEY SQUARE

By CHARLIE PARKER

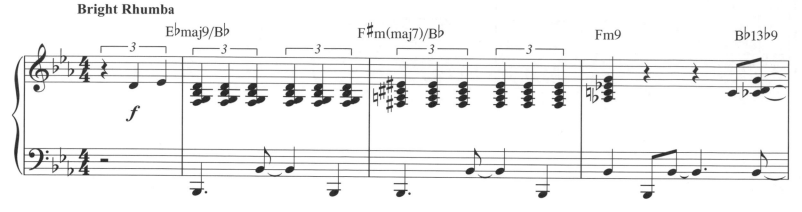

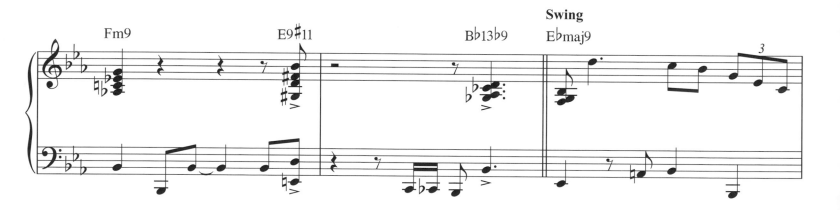

Copyright © 1958 (Renewed 1986) Atlantic Music Corp.
This arrangement Copyright © 2016 Atlantic Music Corp.
International Copyright Secured   All Rights Reserved

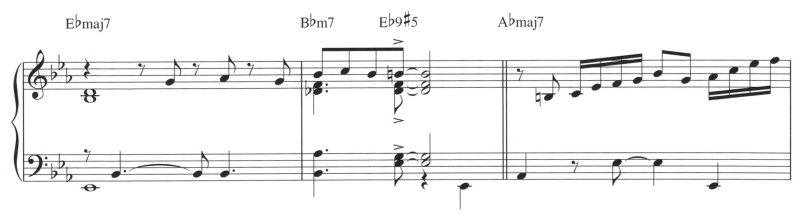

Solo based on one by Charlie Parker

DONNA LEE

By CHARLIE PARKER

Up-tempo Swing

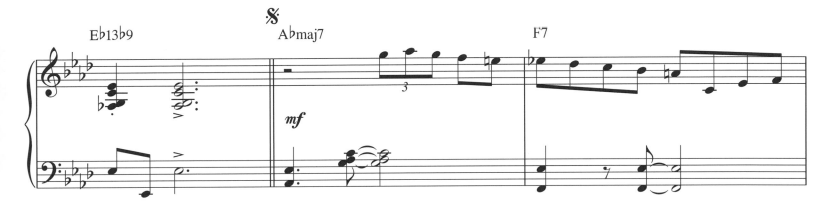

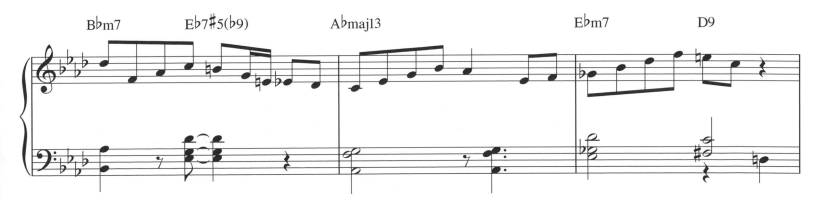

Copyright © 1947 (Renewed 1975) Atlantic Music Corp.
This arrangement Copyright © 2016 Atlantic Music Corp.
All Rights for the World excluding the U.S. Controlled and Administered by Screen Gems-EMI Music Inc.
International Copyright Secured   All Rights Reserved

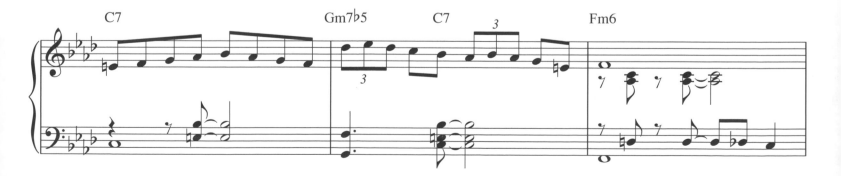

Solo based on one by Charlie Parker

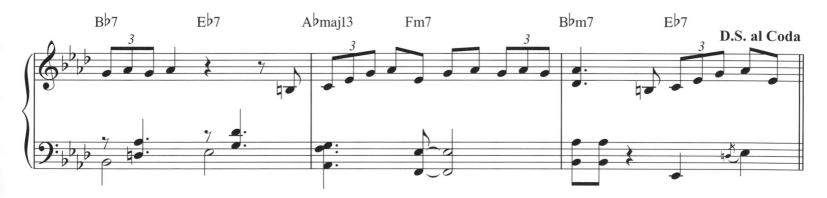

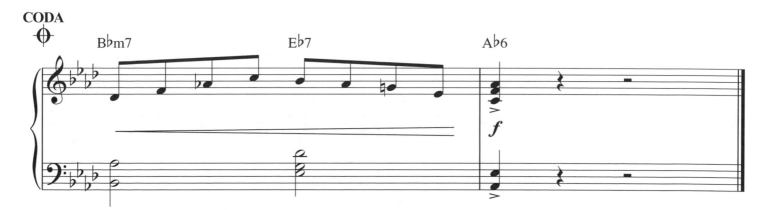

THE GYPSY

Words and Music by
BILLY REID

Arrangement based on one performed by Charlie Parker

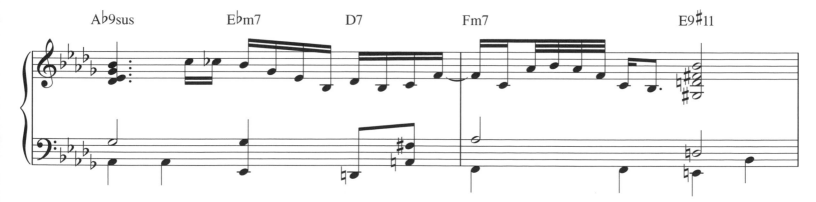

Copyright © 1945 UNIVERSAL MUSIC CORP. and PETER MAURICE MUSIC CO. LTD.
Copyright Renewed
This arrangement Copyright © 2016 UNIVERSAL MUSIC CORP. and PETER MAURICE MUSIC CO. LTD.
All Rights for the U.S. and Canada Controlled and Administered by UNIVERSAL MUSIC CORP.
All Rights Reserved   Used by Permission

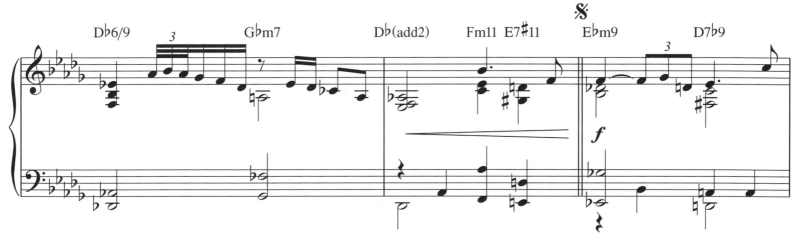

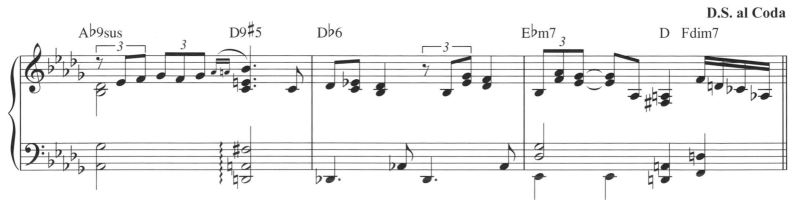

MOOSE THE MOOCHE

By CHARLIE PARKER

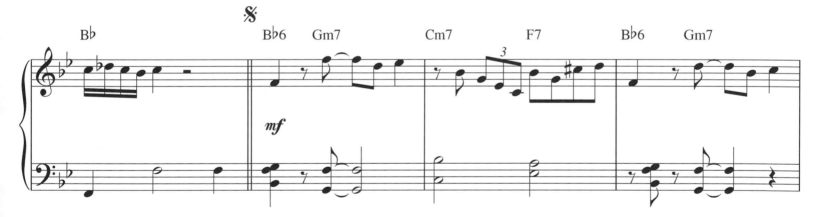

Copyright © 1946 (Renewed 1974) Atlantic Music Corp.
This arrangement Copyright © 2016 Atlantic Music Corp.
International Copyright Secured   All Rights Reserved

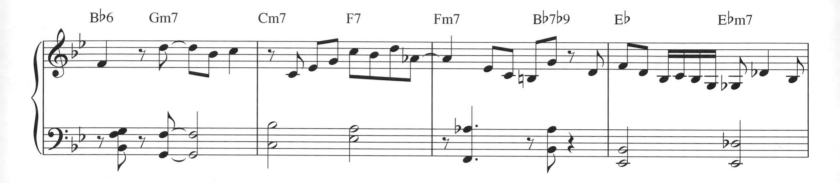

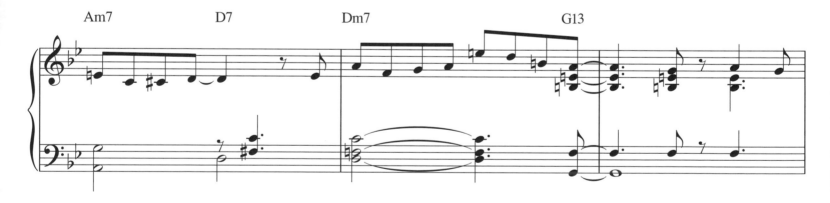

To Coda ⊕

Solo based on one by Charlie Parker

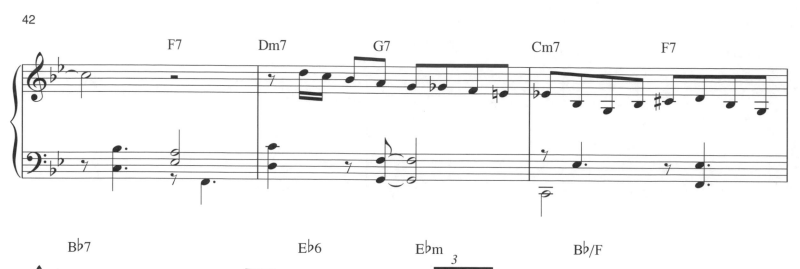

43

JUST FRIENDS

Lyrics by SAM M. LEWIS
Music by JOHN KLENNER

© 1931 (Renewed) METRO-GOLDWYN-MAYER, INC.
This arrangement © 2016 METRO-GOLDWYN-MAYER, INC.
All Rights Controlled by EMI ROBBINS CATALOG INC. (Publishing) and ALFRED MUSIC (Print)
All Rights Reserved   Used by Permission

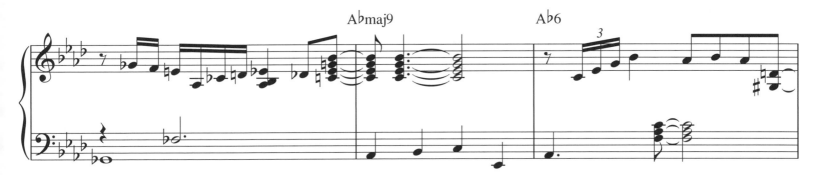

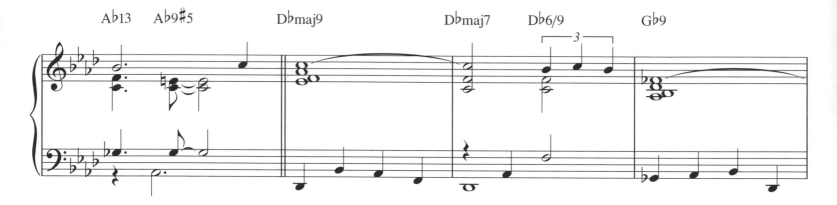

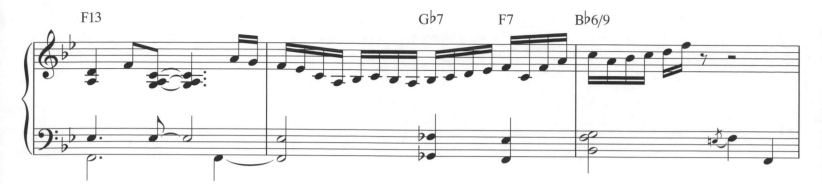

LOVER MAN
(Oh, Where Can You Be?)

Words and Music by JIMMY DAVIS,
ROGER RAMIREZ and JIMMY SHERMAN

Ballad, Swing 8ths

Arrangement based on one performed by Charlie Parker

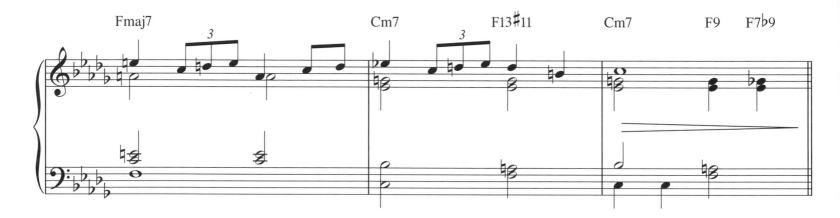

Copyright © 1941, 1942 UNIVERSAL MUSIC CORP.
Copyright Renewed
This arrangement Copyright © 2016 UNIVERSAL MUSIC CORP.
All Rights Reserved   Used by Permission

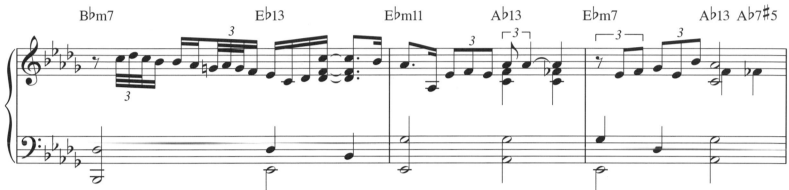

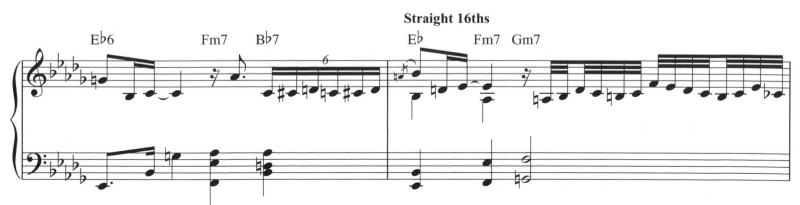

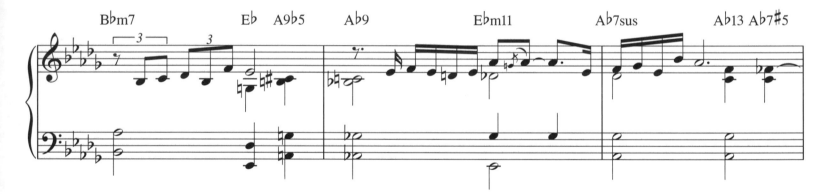

53

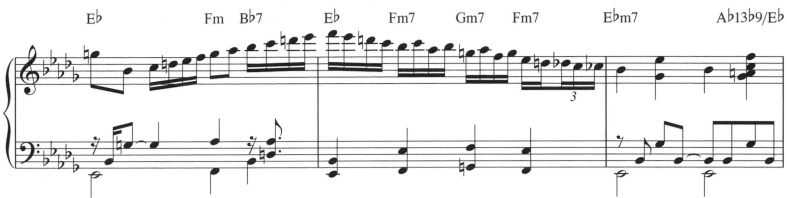

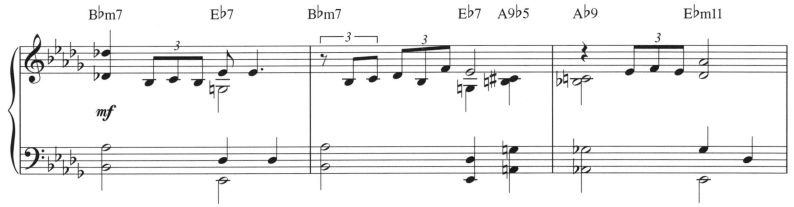

MY LITTLE SUEDE SHOES

By CHARLIE PARKER

Moderate Latin groove

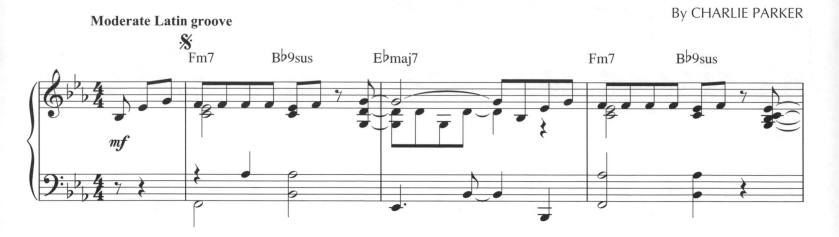

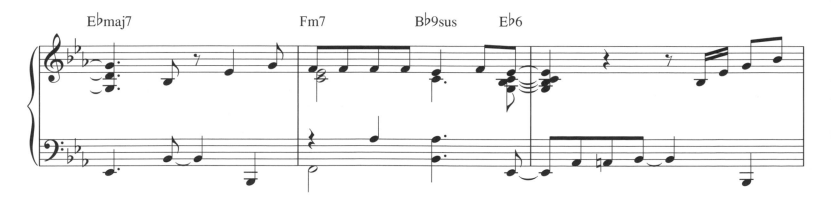

Copyright © 1956 (Renewed 1984) Atlantic Music Corp.
This arrangement Copyright © 2016 Atlantic Music Corp.
International Copyright Secured   All Rights Reserved

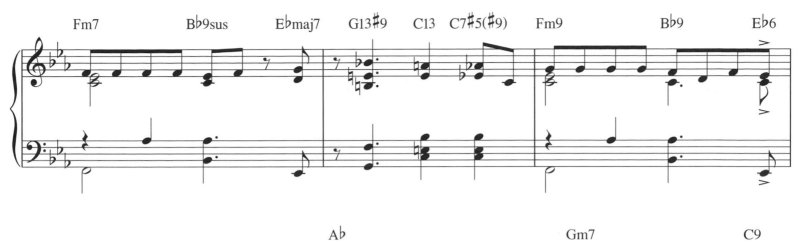

To Coda ⊕

Solo based on one by Charlie Parker

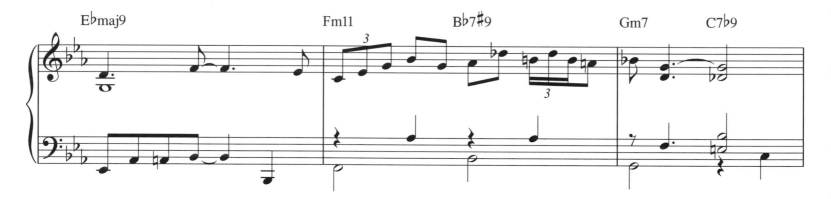

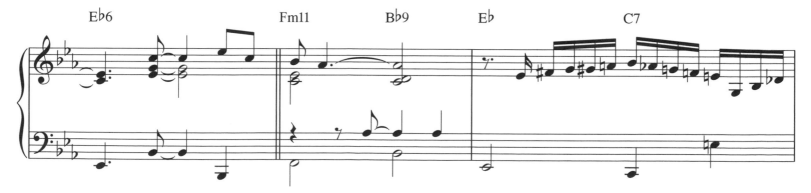

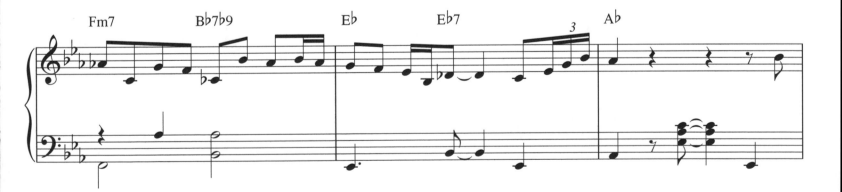

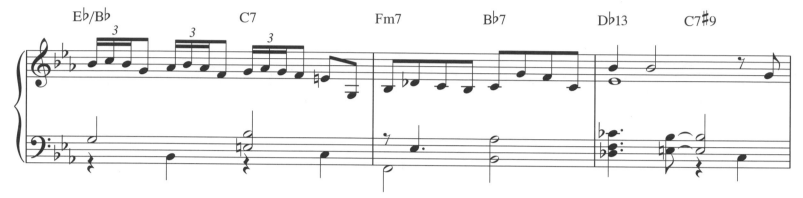

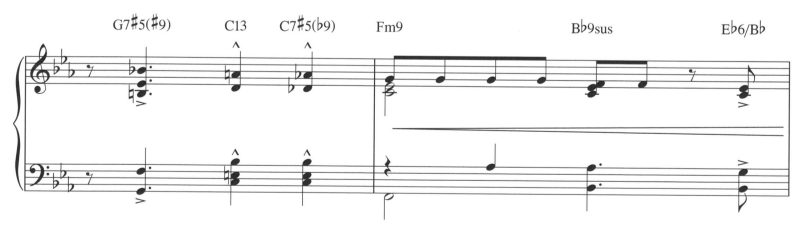

NOW'S THE TIME

By CHARLIE PARKER

Bright Swing

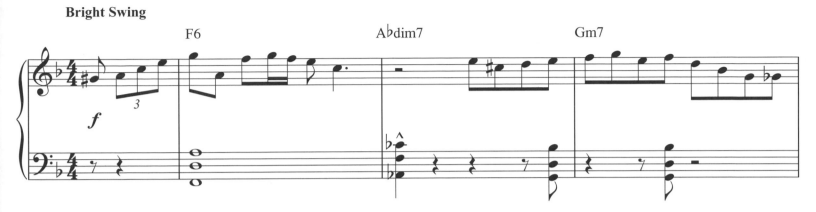

Copyright © 1945 (Renewed 1973) Atlantic Music Corp.
This arrangement Copyright © 2016 Atlantic Music Corp.
All Rights for the World excluding the U.S. Controlled and Administered by Screen Gems-EMI Music Inc.
International Copyright Secured   All Rights Reserved

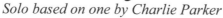

Solo based on one by Charlie Parker

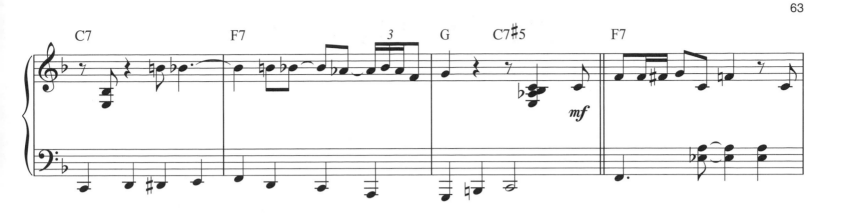

ORNITHOLOGY

By CHARLIE PARKER
and BENNIE HARRIS

Bright Swing

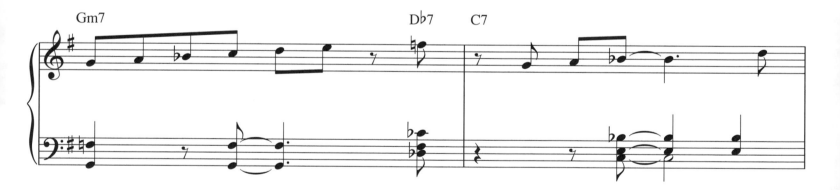

Copyright © 1946 (Renewed 1974) Atlantic Music Corp.
This arrangement Copyright © 2016 Atlantic Music Corp.
International Copyright Secured   All Rights Reserved

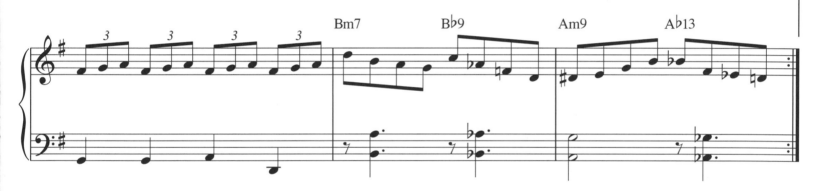

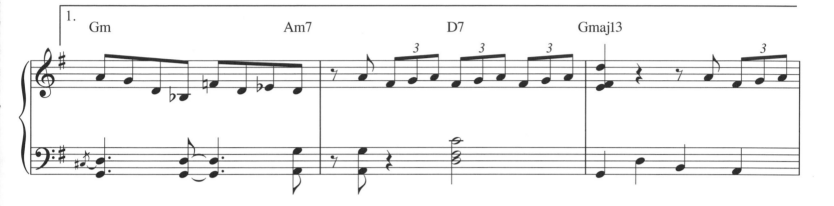

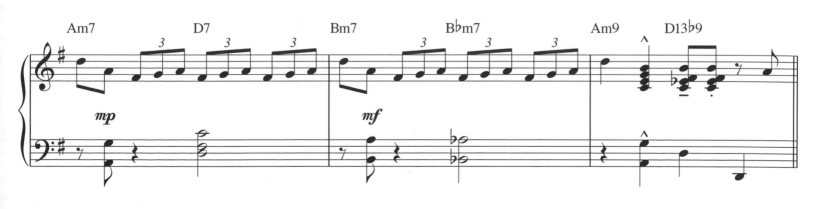

Solo based on one by Charlie Parker

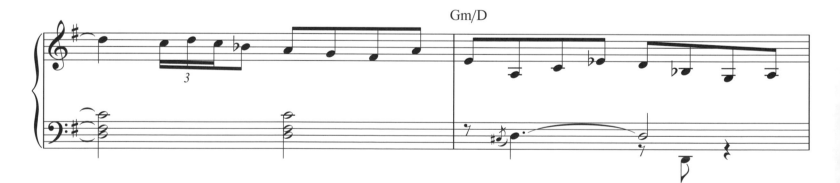

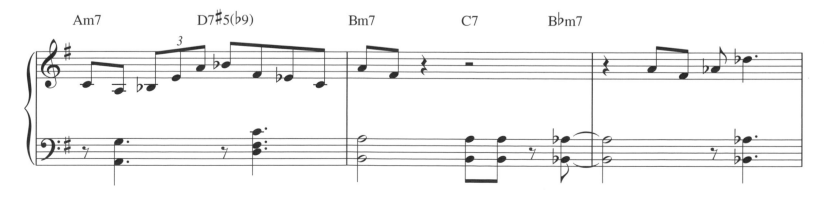

68

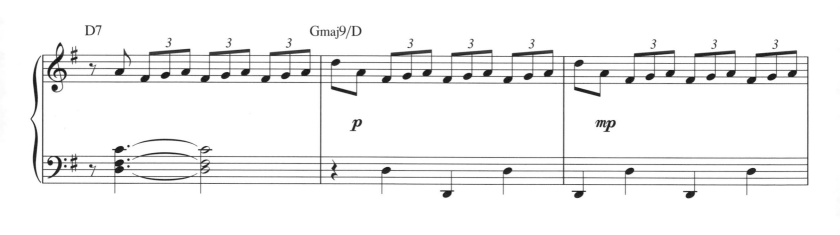

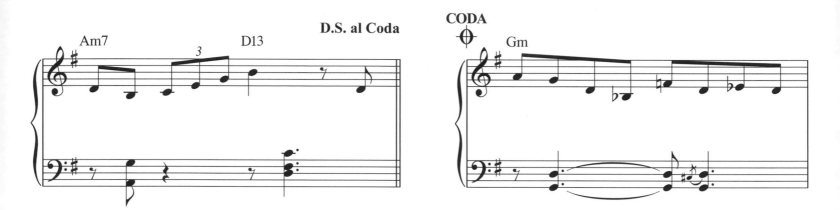

OUT OF NOWHERE
from the Paramount Picture DUDE RANCH

Words by EDWARD HEYMAN
Music by JOHNNY GREEN

Freely

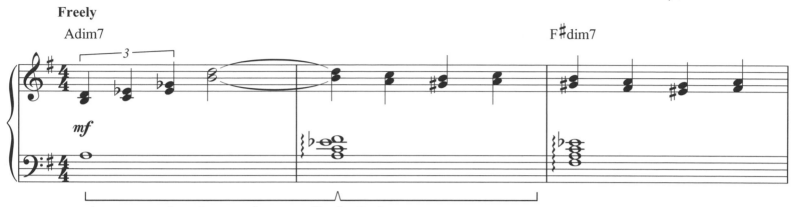

Arrangement based on one featuring Charlie Parker

Moderate Swing

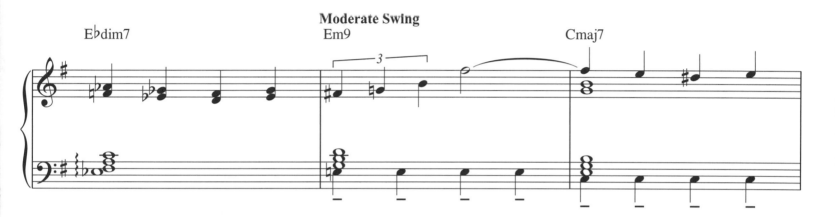

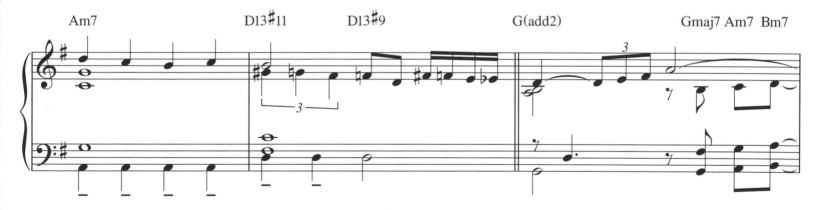

Copyright © 1931 Sony/ATV Music Publishing LLC
Copyright Renewed
This arrangement Copyright © 2016 Sony/ATV Music Publishing LLC
All Rights Administered by Sony/ATV Music Publishing LLC, 424 Church Street, Suite 1200, Nashville, TN 37219
International Copyright Secured All Rights Reserved

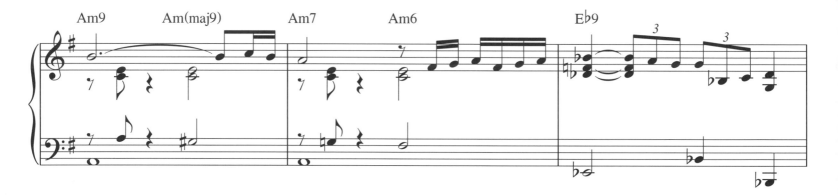

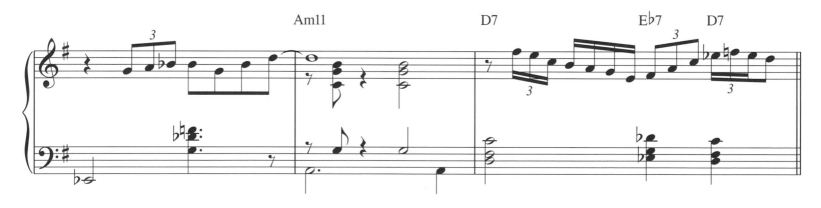

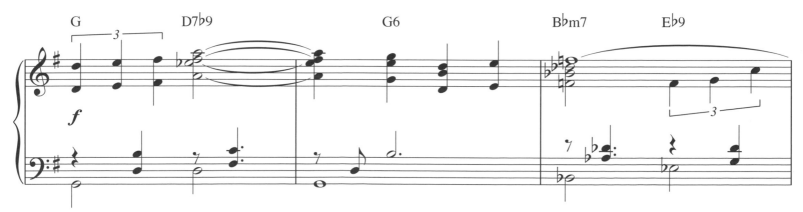

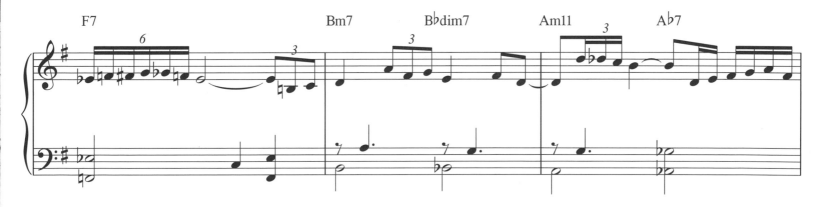

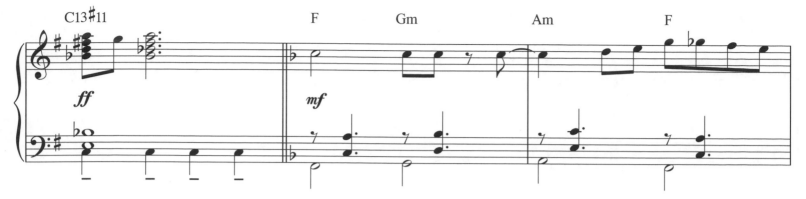

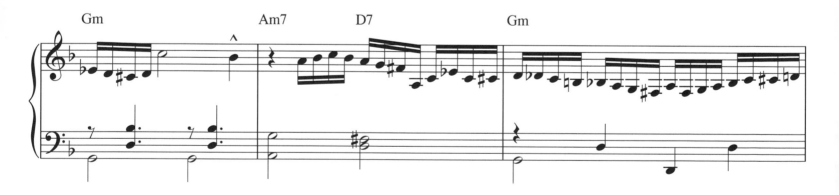

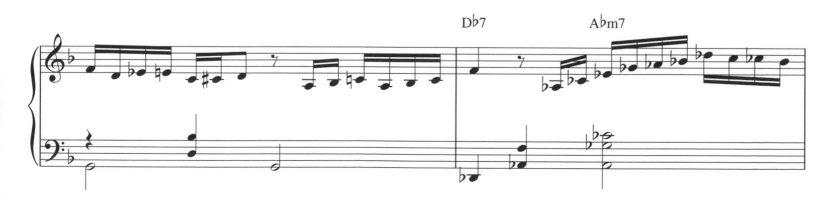

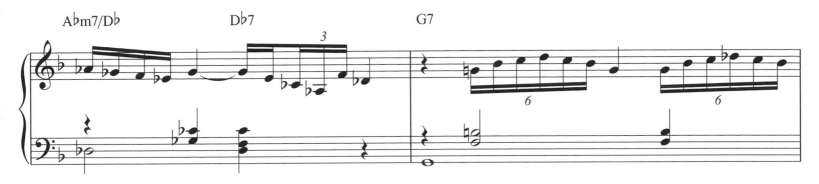

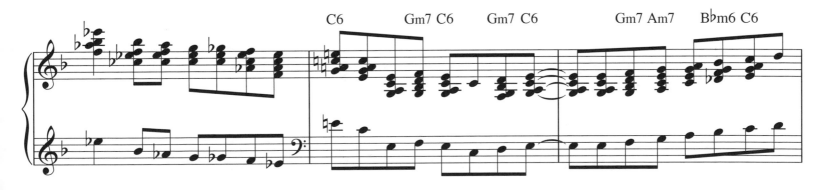

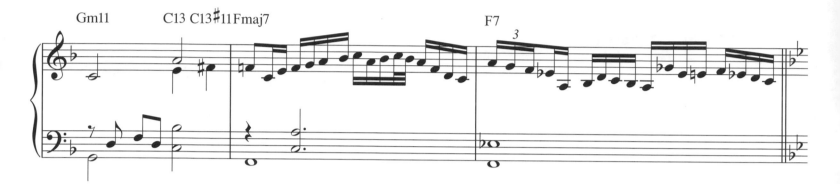

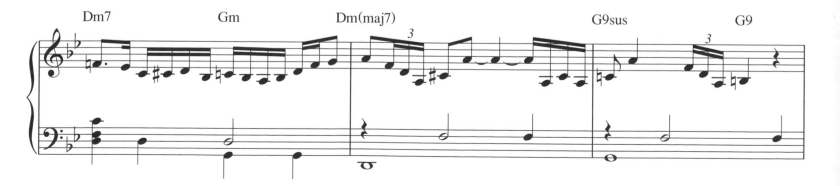

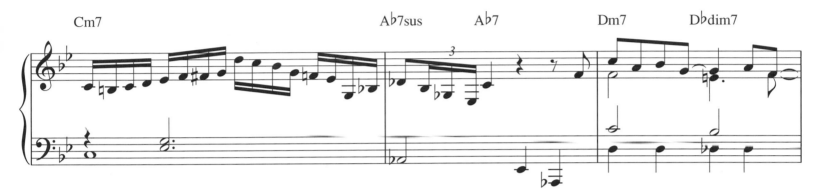

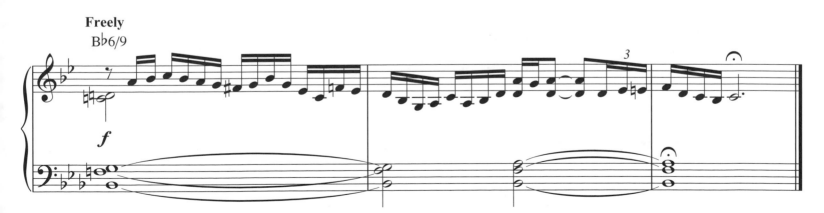

PARKER'S MOOD

By CHARLIE PARKER

Arrangement based on one performed by Charlie Parker

Copyright © 1948 Atlantic Music Corp.
Copyright Renewed and Assigned 1976 Atlantic Music Corp.
This arrangement Copyright © 2016 Atlantic Music Corp.
All Rights for the World excluding the U.S. Controlled and Administered by Screen Gems-EMI Music Inc.
International Copyright Secured   All Rights Reserved

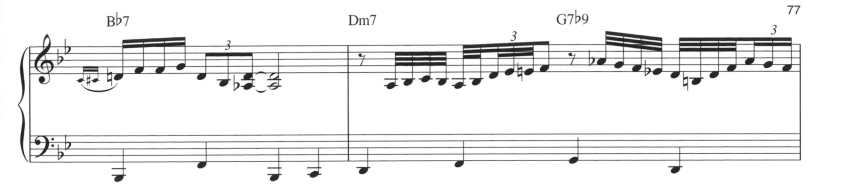

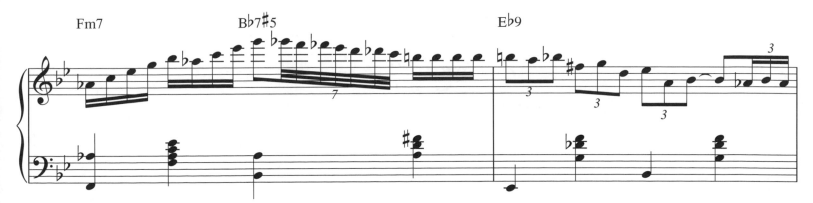

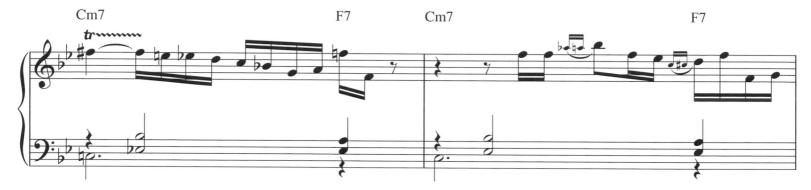

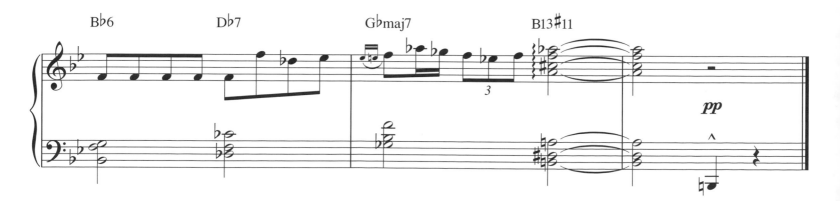

RELAXIN' AT THE CAMARILLO

By CHARLIE PARKER

Bright Swing

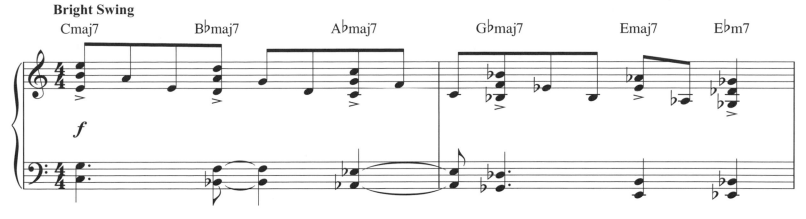

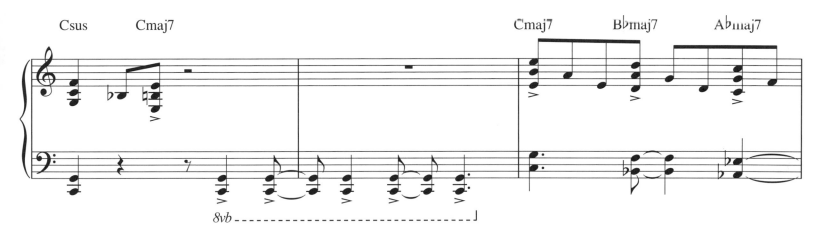

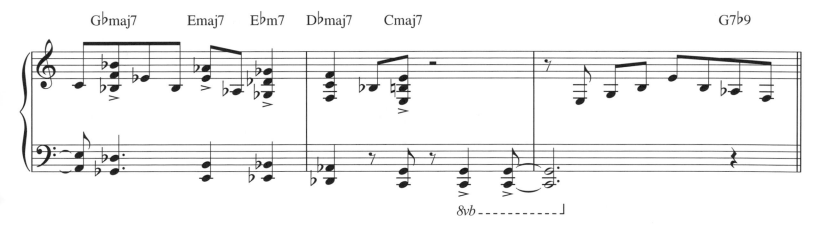

Copyright © 1961 SONGS OF UNIVERSAL, INC.
Copyright Renewed
This arrangement Copyright © 2016 SONGS OF UNIVERSAL, INC.
All Rights Reserved   Used by Permission

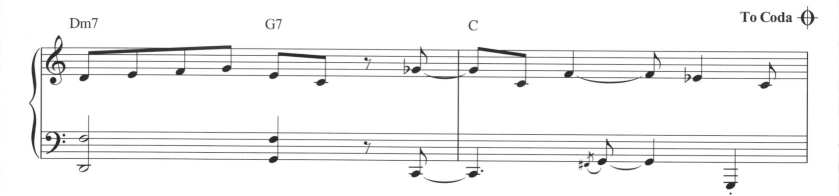

*Solo based on ones by Charlie Parker
and Dodo Marmarosa*

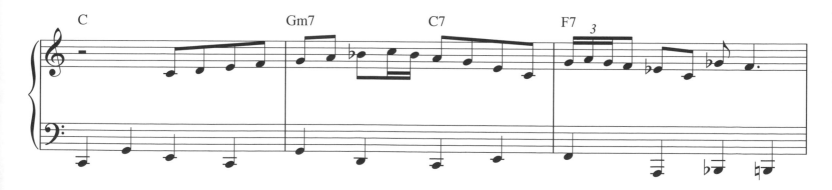

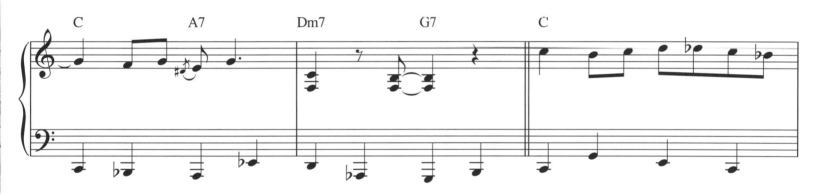

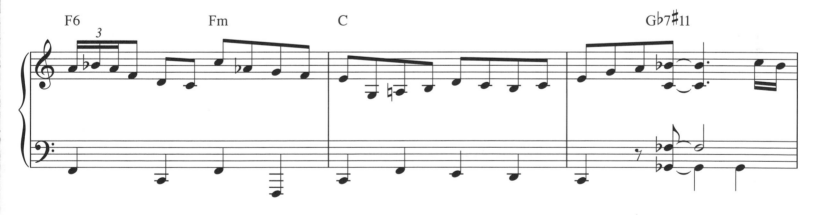

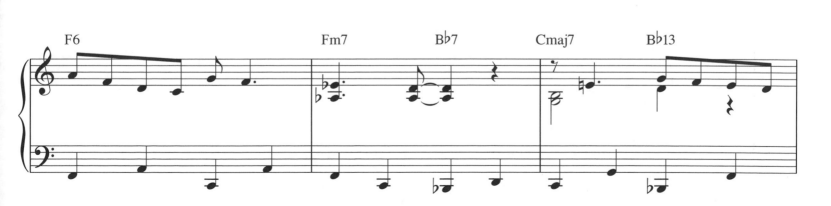

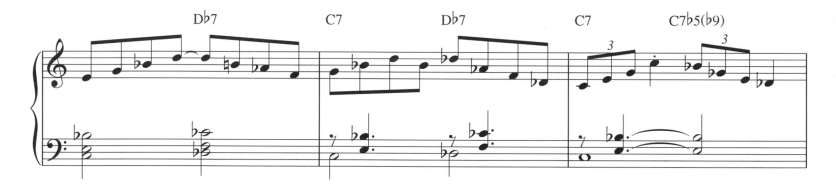

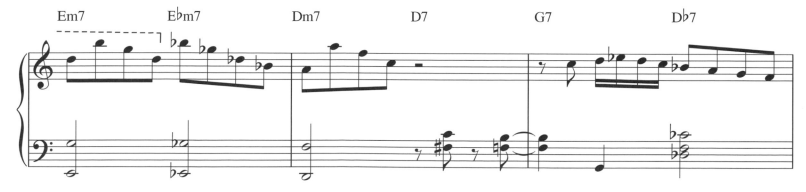

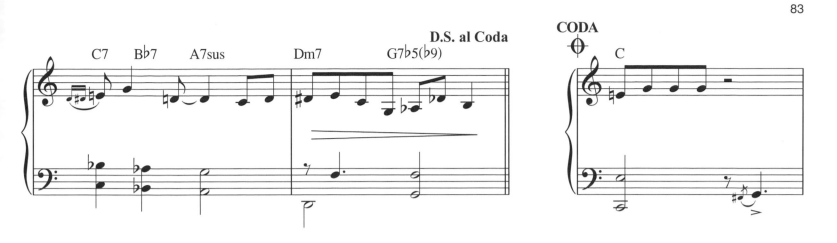

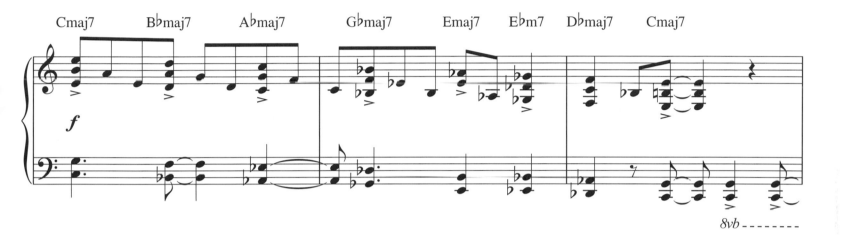

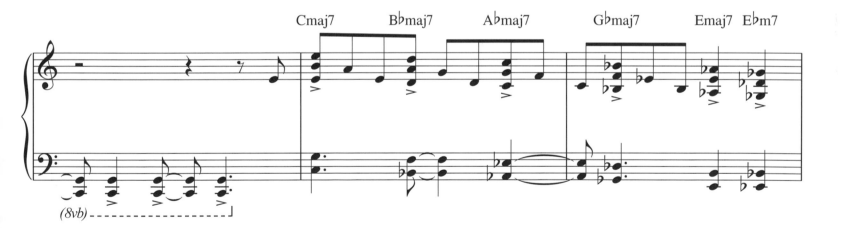

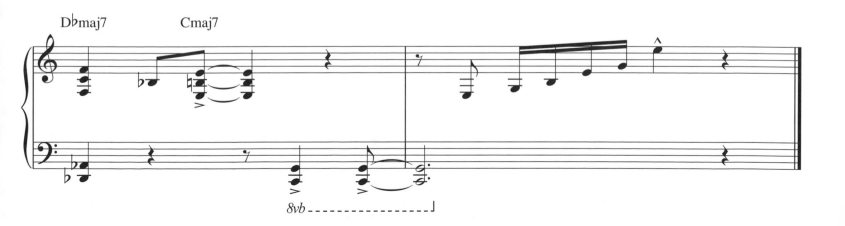

SCRAPPLE FROM THE APPLE

By CHARLIE PARKER

Medium Bop

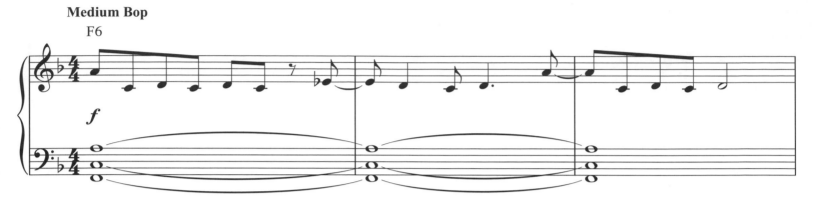

Copyright © 1957 (Renewed 1985) Atlantic Music Corp.
This arrangement Copyright © 2016 Atlantic Music Corp.
International Copyright Secured   All Rights Reserved

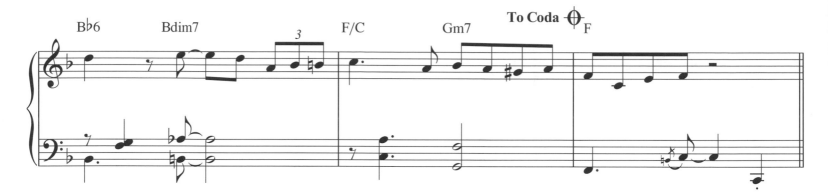

Solo based on one by Charlie Parker

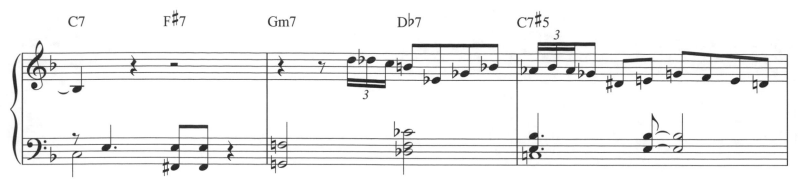

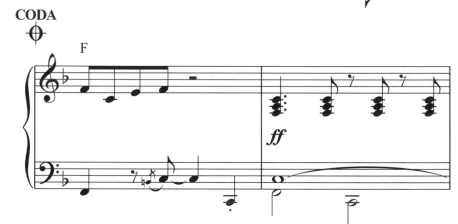

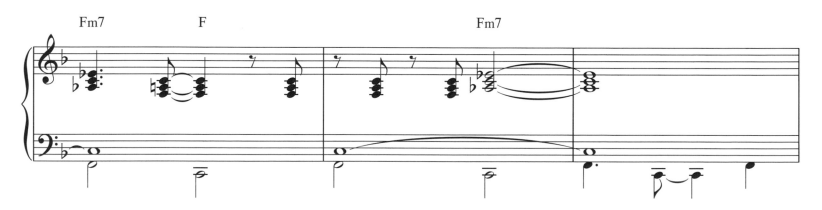

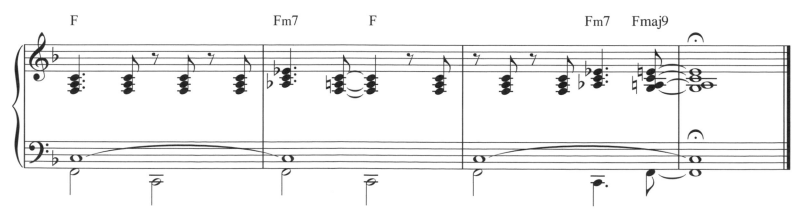

SUMMERTIME
from PORGY AND BESS ®

Music and Lyrics by GEORGE GERSHWIN,
DuBOSE and DOROTHY HEYWARD
and IRA GERSHWIN

© 1935 (Renewed) NOKAWI MUSIC, FRANKIE G. SONGS, DUBOSE AND DOROTHY HEYWARD MEMORIAL FUND PUBLISHING and IRA GERSHWIN MUSIC
This arrangement © 2016 NOKAWI MUSIC, FRANKIE G. SONGS, DUBOSE AND DOROTHY HEYWARD MEMORIAL FUND PUBLISHING and IRA GERSHWIN MUSIC
All Rights for NOKAWI MUSIC Administered by IMAGEM SOUNDS
All Rights for FRANKIE G. SONGS and DUBOSE AND DOROTHY HEYWARD MEMORIAL FUND PUBLISHING Administered by SONGS MUSIC PUBLISHING
All Rights for IRA GERSHWIN MUSIC Administered by WB MUSIC CORP.
All Rights Reserved   Used by Permission

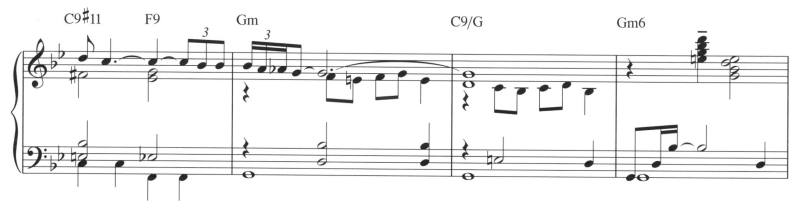

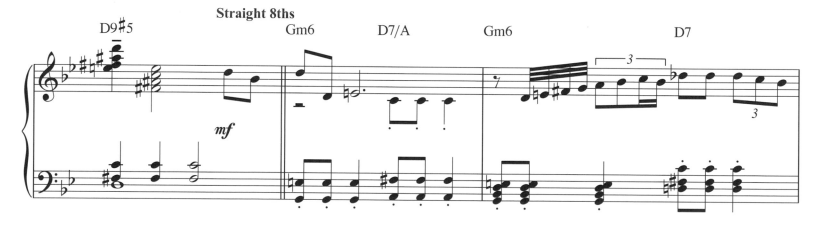

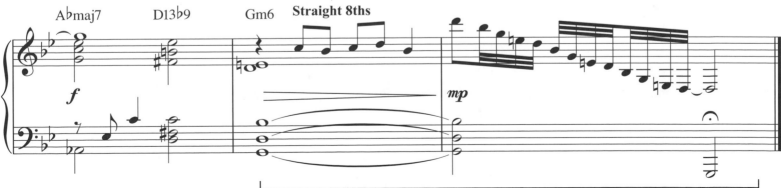

YARDBIRD SUITE

By CHARLIE PARKER

Bright Swing

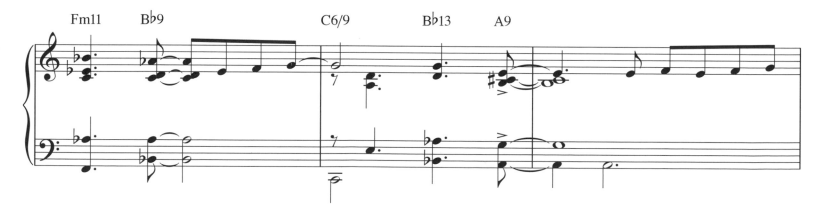

Copyright © 1946 ATLANTIC MUSIC CORP.
Copyright Renewed
This arrangement Copyright © 2016 ATLANTIC MUSIC CORP.
All Rights Reserved   Used by Permission

93

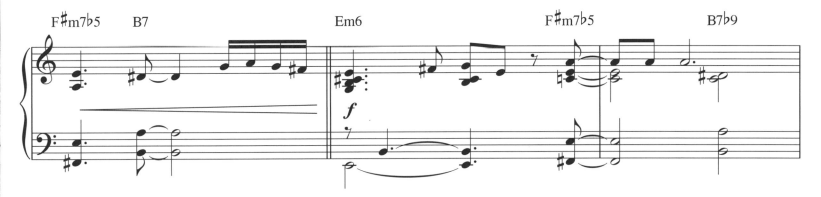

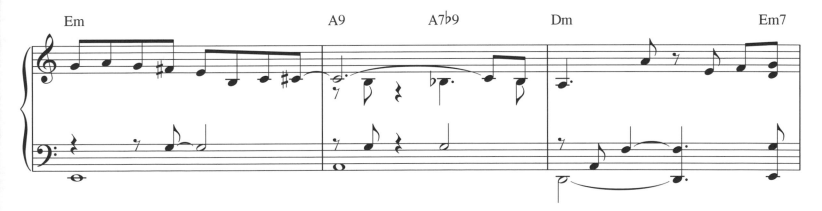

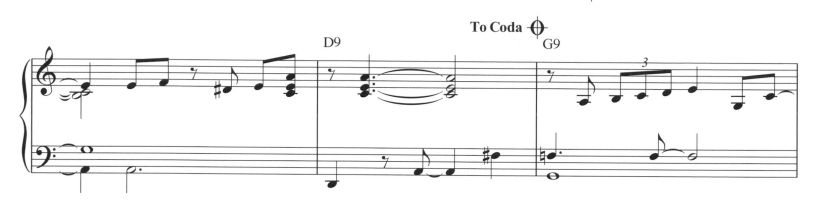

Solo based on one by Charlie Parker

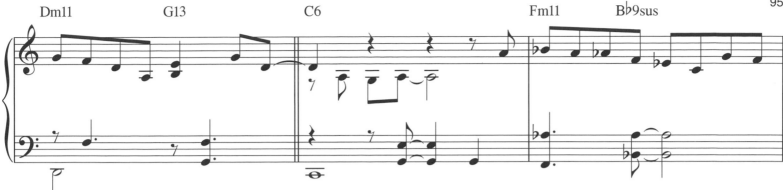

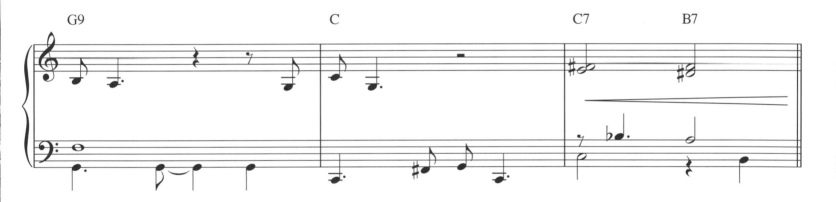

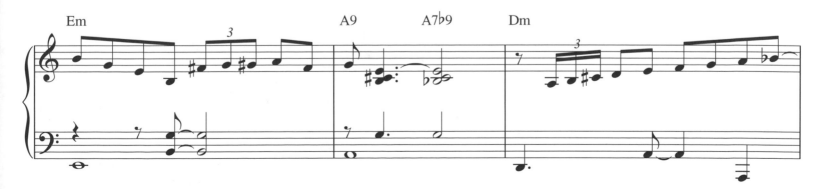

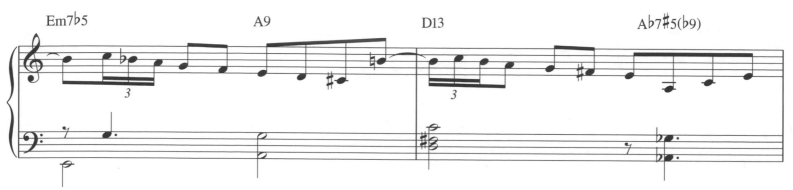

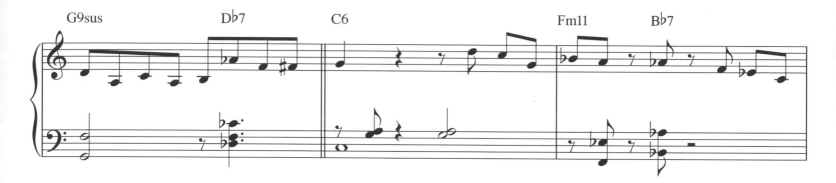

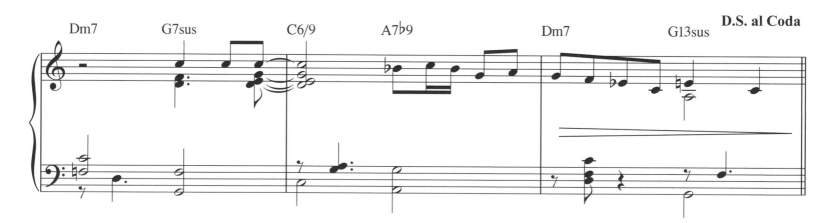

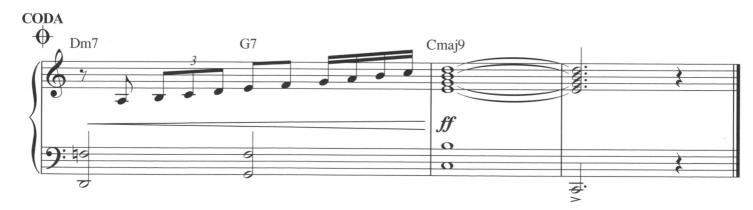